# SMALL WORLD

## SENIOR AUTHORS
Virginia A. Arnold
Carl B. Smith

## LITERATURE CONSULTANTS
Joan I. Glazer
Margaret H. Lippert

READING EXPRESS
MACMILLAN

Macmillan Publishing Company
New York

Collier Macmillan Publishers
London

# ACKNOWLEDGMENTS

*The publisher gratefully acknowledges permission to reprint the following copyrighted material:*

"The Bears on Hemlock Mountain" is adapted from THE BEARS ON HEMLOCK MOUNTAIN by Alice Dalgliesh. Copyright 1952 Alice Dalgliesh; copyright renewed 1980 Margaret Evans. Reprinted with the permission of Charles Scribner's Sons.

"It's A Small World" by Richard M. Sherman and Robert B. Sherman. © 1963 Wonderland Music Co., Inc. International Copyright secured. All Rights Reserved. Used by permission of Wonderland Music Company, Inc.

"Storm" from THE THINGS THAT ARE by Adrien Stoutenberg. Copyright © 1965 by Adrien Stoutenberg. Reprinted by permission of Curtis Brown, Ltd.

"The Turtle" from ZOO DOINGS by Jack Prelutsky. Copyright © 1970, 1980 by Jack Prelutsky. By permission of Greenwillow Books (A Division of William Morrow & Company).

"Winter Walk" (text) from IN ONE DOOR AND OUT THE OTHER: A Book of Poems by Aileen Fisher (Thomas Y. Crowell). Copyright © 1969 by Aileen Fisher. By permission of Harper & Row, Publishers, Inc.

**Cover Design:** Bass and Goldman Associates

**Illustration Credits:** Mary Balsman, 134–142; Andrea Baruffi, 84–92; Janet Colby, 65; Carolyn Croll, 20–29; Lulu Delacre, 93; Dennis DiVincenzo, 124–125; Jerry Dodds, 194–195; Susan Dodge, 66, 94, 114–115, 126, 156–157, 164, 184; Andrea Eberbach, 206–209, 211–213, 215–217; Len Ebert, 74–81; Barbara Lanza, 44–53; Tom Leonard, 198, 200–202, 204; Sal Murdocca, 104–111; Michelle Noiset, 30–41; Ed Parker, 10–19; Paul Pugliese, 131; Denise Hilton Putnam, 174–183; David Rose, 218–227; Samantha Smith, 56–64; Susan Snider, 116–122; Dave Taylor, 144–147, 149–152; Lorna Tomei, 229–239.

**Cover Photo:** The Image Bank: © E. Lewin

**Photo Credits:** Bruce Coleman, Inc.: © Eric Carle, 161; © David Madison, 25; © David Overcash, 186MR; © Mike Price, 186MM; © Ronald F. Thomas, 24. Colour Library International Ltd. 99R; © Phil Degginger, 97R. © Tina Enghoff/Kent Klich, 167–169, 173. The Image Bank, 8; © Brett Froomer, 189; © Gabe Palmer, 99L. © Buck Miller, 165, 170–173. Leo de Wys: Danilo Boschung, 112. Monkmeyer Press Photo Service, Inc.: © Murray Greenburgh, 192; © Hugh Rogers, 98, 160; NASA, 26. NOAA, 72. Photo Researchers, Inc.: © Bill Bachman, 97L; © Jules Bucher, 25; © Van Bucher, 23; © Barbara Burnes, 186TR; © James Hanley, 186BM; © Richard Hutchings, 95; © Paolo Koch, 190; © Susan McCartney, 161; © Will McIntyre, 186TL; © Lawrence Migdale, 27. © Porterfield/Chickering, 186BR. © R. Rowan, 186BL; © C. Vergara, 185, 186BR; Larry Voight, 193; © Ernst A. Weber, 188; © Myron Wood, 25, 186TM; Shostal Associates, Inc.: 67, 70. © Louis Van Camp, 24. © Eric Simonsen, 72. Tom Stack & Associates: © Brian Parker, 100. Starwood: © Lelia Hendren, 127. Stock, Boston: © Dan Brody, 28. © Patrick Ward, 162. © Lee White, 96, 158, 166. U.S. Department of Commerce, 68. © Carl Zitzman, 128–129, 130, 132.

Macmillan Publishing Company
866 Third Avenue
New York, N.Y. 10022
Collier Macmillan Canada, Inc.

Printed in the United States of America

ISBN 0-02-160070-8

9  8  7  6

# Contents

# RAIN
# OR
# SHINE

# PREPARING FOR READING

## Learning Vocabulary

Listen.

<u>s</u>trange things

Read.

1. A <u>strong</u> wind blew in the woods.
2. The <u>weather</u> didn't look good.
3. The family didn't like <u>camping</u> in the <u>rain</u>.
4. The family couldn't sleep with the <u>noise</u> of the wind and rain on the tent.

strong    weather    camping
rain    noise

## Developing Background

Read and talk.

### Camping Trips

Camping trips can be very special, but first you must get ready to go. What do you take on camping trips? You don't know what the weather will be, so be ready for sun or rain. You will want to take food and a tent. Is that all you will take? What will you do on your trips? In *A Night in the Woods*, a family likes to go on camping trips. What are the yellow blinking eyes by the tent?

# A Night In The Woods

Susan J. Shillcock

David was very happy. He was camping with his family in the woods. He said to his mother and father, "I know I will like camping in the woods. The wind will help me go to sleep. There is so much to do when we are camping! I hope we can go swimming, and take a long walk in the woods, and go on a picnic, too."

"We can do many things, but I hope it doesn't rain," said Father. "Right now it's time for us to get ready for bed."

David called to his little brother, "Come on, Paul! It's bedtime! Come into the tent now!"

"I am coming right now," Paul said. "Wait for me! I am a little scared of sleeping in the woods."

David said, "Don't be scared. I will take care of you. I will read you a story. I know that will help."

"You may read one story, but then go right to sleep," said Mother.

"Good night!" they all called.

David read Paul a story of a very small bear cub in the woods. The story did help Paul. He could not stop laughing at the funny pictures. He was not so scared of sleeping in the woods now.

David was happy he could help his brother. "It's time to be quiet now and to go to sleep," he said. "That noise out there is the strong wind in the woods. Rain might be coming. Don't be scared of the weather."

Paul said, "I hope it doesn't rain. We can't go on a picnic in the rain, and I want to look for the bear in your book."

"Go to sleep now," said David.

David and Paul were very quiet. Then Paul said, "David, I am not scared of the rain or the strong wind. But I *am* scared. I see something. Do you see it, too? Something is out there, looking in at us."

David looked out into the black night. He couldn't see it at first. He looked and looked. Then he saw it! It *did* look like something was looking at them. There were two yellow eyes blinking by their tent. David did not know what it could be. He was big and strong, but he was scared, too!

There was little noise but the noise of the wind. David and Paul looked at the yellow eyes. The yellow eyes looked at David and Paul. "I am scared," said Paul. "Is it a bear? I want Mother and Father. I want to go home."

David was scared, too, but he said, "I will take care of you. It may be a fox or a rabbit looking for food. It's raining now. It will go away in the rain."

David was happy to see the rain. In this weather the something with the big yellow eyes should go home. But the big yellow eyes did not go away. Why didn't they go away? David and Paul were very scared.

Then Mother called to David and Paul "It's time to stop the noise and go to sleep."

"Mother," David called. "Something is looking in at us. We both see big yellow eyes blinking at us. Will you see what it is?"

Mother said, "Don't be scared. We will see what it is right now."

David and Paul looked out into the black night. They saw Mother and Father go over to the big yellow eyes. Then Mother and Father were laughing. Why were they laughing?

"Look at this, David and Paul," said Father. "It's not raining now, so you can come out of the tent. Come and see what the big yellow eyes are." When David and Paul saw what the big yellow eyes were, they were not scared.

Mother said, "Some things do look strange at night, when you are camping. We should let your friends go now. Then we can all get some sleep!"

# Questions

Read and think.
1. What did David do to help Paul go to sleep?
2. Why did David and Paul get scared when they looked out of their tent?
3. Why was David happy when the rain came?
4. Who helped David and Paul see what was scary?

# PREPARING FOR READING

## Learning Vocabulary

Listen.

c<u>ow</u>                    m<u>ou</u>se

Read.

1. <u>How</u> can you <u>tell</u> what the weather will be?

2. Some people turn on the <u>radio</u> or <u>TV</u>.

3. You can see a <u>storm</u> on the weather <u>map</u> on TV.

| how | tell | radio |
| --- | --- | --- |
| TV | storm | map |

## Developing Background

Read and talk.

## A Weather Forecast

The Miller family likes to do things
together. They want to go camping and ride
in their boat, but they don't want to go in the
rain. They need a weather forecast. A
weather forecast will tell them what the
weather may be. Where can they get a
forecast? They might get one on radio or TV.
In *What Will the Weather Be?*, you can read
what forecasters do to put together a
weather forecast.

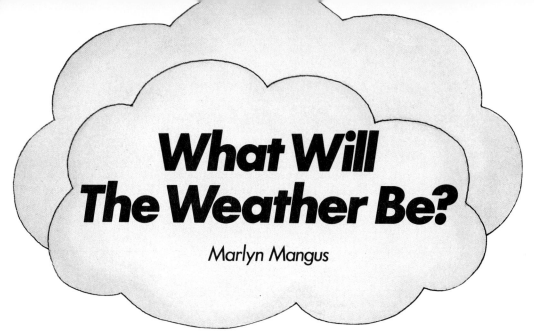

# What Will The Weather Be?

### Marlyn Mangus

What will the weather be? We all want to know. People who farm need to know. People who fly a plane need to know. People who drive a truck need to know. You and I want to know.

Will it storm or rain? Will it be a good day for a picnic? Will it be hot or cold? What should we put on?

People on TV and radio tell us what the weather is like now. They can forecast the weather, too. They can tell us what kind of weather we will have. We can get ready for a storm, a rain, or a strong wind.

The people who forecast the weather are called weather forecasters. Many things make up the weather. What can weather forecasters tell us? How do they know what the day will be like?

The air around us helps make up the weather. Weather forecasters look at this instrument to know what the air is like.

Barometer

Thermometer

The weather forecasters want to know how hot or cold the air is. This is the instrument they use to tell.

Forecasters want to know how much rain is falling. Look at the picture. Rain will fall into this instrument. This instrument helps tell us how much rain there is.

Rain Gauge

Hygrometer

You know there is water in the air when it is raining. There is water in the air when it is not raining, too. Forecasters read this instrument to tell how much water is in the air.

How strong is the wind? Where is it coming from? Forecasters look at the instruments in the pictures to tell what the wind is like.

Weather Vane

Anemometer

Weather forecasters look at the clouds. Clouds come from water in the air. Clouds help forecasters tell when we will have a storm.

Satellites, too, help weather forecasters tell what the weather will be. From high up, satellites take pictures. The pictures show where there are clouds. They show where it is raining and where there is a storm. They show where the sky is blue and where the weather is good.

Now the weather forecasters can make a map. The map will show what the weather is like all over the country.

Weather forecasters look at a new weather map each day. They can tell where the weather will move. They can tell where there will be a storm or a strong wind.

Now the people on TV and radio can tell us what the weather is like where we are. They can read some of the weather instruments. They can show us a weather map or pictures from satellites, too. They can tell us what the weather will be where we are. Then we can be ready when we go out.

What will the weather be? Turn on the TV or the radio. The weather forecasters can help us know what kind of day we will have.

# Questions

Read and think.

1. What are the people who forecast the weather called?
2. What instrument can tell how hot or cold the air is?
3. What does a weather map show?

# PREPARING FOR READING

## Learning Vocabulary

Listen.

cow                    mouse

Read.

1. The forecast said the rain might last for an hour.
2. Thunder came with the rain.
3. If the boy and girl had to go out in the rain, they could get very wet.
4. The children didn't like to be alone in the storm.

| hour | thunder | if |
|------|---------|-----|
| had  | wet     | alone |

## Developing Background

Read and talk.

March 8, 1988

Dear David,

   My sister and I had a strange time last night. First of all, there was a storm with rain, thunder, and lightning. Then the man on TV said a bear was missing from the zoo. On top of all that, the lights blew out. Maria says to tell you that she will write a play for school called *The Missing Bear*. It will tell the story of that night.

Your friend,
Carmen

# THE MISSING BEAR

**Michael Dayton**

---

**The Players**

**Carmen    Paco    Maria    A Man on TV**

---

*(Carmen and Maria are looking at TV with their brother Paco.)*

**Man on TV:** Now it is time for the weather forecast. The forecast calls for rain in the next hour. We will get some thunder and lightning, too. And now for the last story. A black bear is missing from the zoo.

**Maria:** A bear is missing from the zoo?

**Man on TV:** That's right, friends. A bear is missing from the zoo. People from the zoo are looking for it. And now, good night from CXY TV.

**Maria:** That's scary! One time I saw a bear with huge claws on TV.

**Carmen:** Paco, what could we do if the bear came to this house?

**Maria:** We could hide under the bed.

**Paco:** That bear is not coming to this house. The zoo is an hour away by bus. For a bear, that's a long walk.

**Maria:** It is a long walk, but the bear could run.

**Paco:** Why are you two scared? Mother and Father are home.

**Carmen:** I am not scared at all. If that bear does come, I will step on its foot. Then that bear will run like the wind.

**Paco:** If that bear does come to this house, you will fly away like a chicken.

**Carmen:** That's not true.

**Paco:** Why don't you keep an eye out for the bear. I have to read a book for school.

*(Paco walks out.)*

**Maria:** Paco, don't go! Now we are all alone, Carmen.

**Carmen:** Let Paco go, Maria. You weren't scared when you saw the lion at the circus, were you? You should not be scared of a bear.

**Maria:** I was not scared of the lion because it was not missing.

*(There is a little noise.)*

**Carmen:** What was that?

**Maria:** *(laughing)* That was the cat. Now who is scared?

*(There is a big noise. They both jump. The TV and the lights go out.)*

**Maria:** What was that? Why did the lights go out?

**Carmen:** That was thunder. Look! It's raining. Look at the lightning!

**Maria:** This is a scary night. A bear is missing, the lights are out, and now there is a big storm with thunder!

**Carmen:** I am not scared. I like a storm at night.

**Maria:** *(pointing)* Look! Something moved. Something is out there.

**Carmen:** Where? I don't see it.

**Maria:** We will have to wait for the next lightning.

**Maria:** Look! There *is* something strange out there!

**Carmen:** It must be the missing bear. Paco! Mother! Father! Help! Where are they? Maria, we are alone with that bear! Come on!

(*Carmen, Maria, and the cat dive under the bed.*)

**Carmen:** Didn't you see the bear, Maria?

**Maria:** I don't know. I saw something.

(*Paco runs in and looks under the bed.*)

**Paco:** Mother asked me to see if you two are all right. Why are you under the bed?

**Maria:** Paco, you must hide. Carmen saw the missing bear out there.

**Paco:** Come out from under there. Carmen, you said you weren't scared of that bear. You said you could step on the bear's foot.

**Carmen:** I said that?

*(The TV and the lights come on. Maria and Carmen come from under the bed.)*

**Maria:** The lights are on! Am I happy to see lights!

**Man on TV:** And now for a special story. The missing bear is not missing now.

**Carmen:** What? But I saw it. It was huge. It had big claws, and it had big, black eyes, and . . .

**Man on TV:** In the last hour, the little cub came home to the zoo. It was wet and scared, but it is all right now.

**Maria:** The missing bear was a cub.

**Carmen:** *(pointing)* Paco, look at your sneakers. They are all wet.

**Maria:** I know why his sneakers are wet. When we were alone, he was out in the rain. We saw Paco, not a bear.

**Carmen:** You played a trick on us.

**Paco:** *(laughing)* You are right. I wish I had a picture of you two under the bed. You were pretty scared, weren't you?

**Carmen:** This time we were. Next time a bear is missing, we will jump on his foot like this!

*(Carmen and Maria get ready to jump. Paco runs away.)*

## Questions

Read and think.

1. What was missing from the zoo?
2. What did Carmen and Maria do when they saw something out in the rain?
3. How did Carmen know that Paco was out in the rain?

# WRITING ACTIVITY

## WRITE A TV STORY

### Prewrite

In *The Missing Bear*, the man on CXY TV read a story of a bear missing from the zoo. If you work on TV, you must write the story you will tell on the air. It must be a true story.

You will write a TV story. You may write on one of the trips you will take or did take. You may write on something that is missing. You may write on pets at your school, but write on something you know.

Use the *5 W's* to tell your story.

*Who* or *what* did something?
*Where* was it?
*When* was it?
*Why* did you write on this?

## Write

1. Write your TV story on your paper.
2. Your first sentence should say *who* or *what* did something.
3. Then write sentences that tell *where*, *when*, and *why*.
4. Use your Glossary for help with words.

## Revise

Read your TV story. Did you use the *5 W's* to tell your story? Did you tell all the things you wanted to tell? If not, do it now.

Read with your teacher.

1. Do your sentences begin with capital letters?
2. Did you use the correct end marks?
3. Did you spell words correctly?

# PREPARING FOR READING

## Learning Vocabulary

Listen.

letter

let • ter

ballet    coach    yellow

Read.

1. The wind <u>began</u> to <u>blow</u> in the woods.
2. The wind <u>roared</u>, but it could not blow the boy away.
3. The boy rushed <u>through</u> the woods to get the wind.
4. <u>After</u> he <u>caught</u> the wind, how could he keep it?

began    blow    roared
through    after    caught

## Developing Background

Read and talk.

### A Story Forecast

What will the weather be? You have read in this book that forecasters look at pictures of satellites. They make a map that can tell us what the weather will be. Some people forecast weather by a story they know. This story may have come down from storyteller to storyteller. *The Boy Who Caught the Wind* is a story like that. Can you forecast the weather from this story?

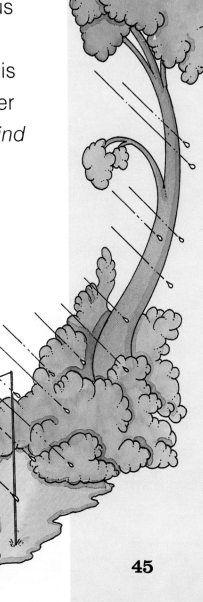

# The Boy Who Caught The Wind

Margaret H. Lippert

When the North Wind blew, it was strong and cold. Day and night it roared over the land. The people were scared of it. They didn't like the North Wind, and they wanted it to stop.

One day a boy and his father were talking in their lodge. "I will stop the North Wind," the boy said.

"How will you do that?" his father asked. "You can't stop something you can't see."

"I must try," said the boy. "May I have some rope and a blanket?" His father gave the boy some rope and a blanket, and the boy walked out of the lodge.

The boy began to walk through the woods. He was looking for a big tree. When he saw a good tree, he put the rope over it. Then he called, "North Wind, come and look at my rope." The North Wind roared over to look at the rope, and blew right through it. When the North Wind blew through the rope, the boy moved fast. He caught the North Wind in his blanket.

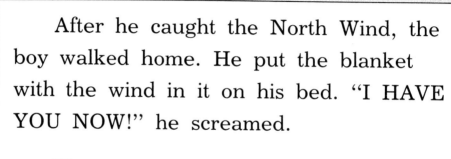

After he caught the North Wind, the boy walked home. He put the blanket with the wind in it on his bed. "I HAVE YOU NOW!" he screamed.

There was so much noise that the people came running. "Why did you scream?" they asked.

"I screamed because I was so happy that I caught the North Wind!" said the boy.

"Where is the wind?" the people asked.

"In my blanket," he said.

"If you have the wind in your blanket, show it to us," said the people.

"I can't show you the wind," said the boy. "If I do, it will get out." The people began talking together. They said the boy didn't have the wind. They said he couldn't have caught the wind. After some time, the boy said, "All right, I *will* show you the wind." He picked up the blanket, and the wind roared out.

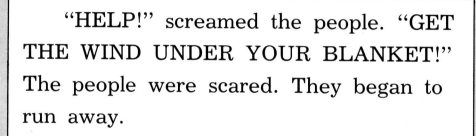

"HELP!" screamed the people. "GET THE WIND UNDER YOUR BLANKET!" The people were scared. They began to run away.

The wind was strong, but it couldn't get out of the lodge. The boy was running all around the lodge after the wind. At last the boy saw the wind duck under his bed. Then the boy drove the wind under his blanket. "Let me out," called the wind through the blanket.

"I will not let you out," said the boy. "You are too strong. You blow day and night. You blow all over the land. All the people are scared of you."

The wind wanted to get out. "If you let me out, I will not blow all the time," he said. "I will let you know when I want to blow."

"How will you do that?" asked the boy.

"Every day when you get up, look at the sky. I will make the sky red when I want to blow. If the sky is red when you get up, let the people know that they must get ready for a storm. They will not have to be scared of me now, because they will know when I am coming." Then the boy let the wind go, and the wind blew up to the sky.

So that is how the boy caught the North Wind, and that is why if you see a red sky when you get up, you, too, will know that you should get ready for a storm.

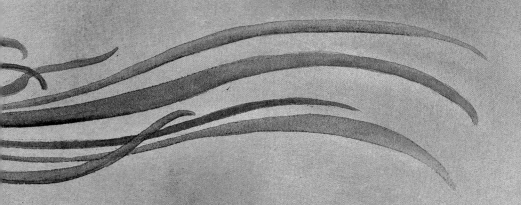

## Questions

Read and think.

1. Why were the people scared of the wind?
2. How did the boy get the wind?
3. Why didn't the boy want to show the people the wind?
4. How could the North Wind show the people that a storm was coming?

# PREPARING FOR READING

## Learning Vocabulary

Listen.

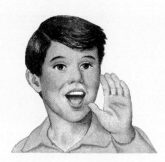

scream

Read.

1. The boat didn't have a <u>scratch</u> after the storm.

2. The man moved it to a quiet <u>place</u> by his house.

scratch    place

## Developing Background

Read and talk.

### How Do I Look?

Many people must have glasses to help them see. Eyes are so special for us that we should take good care of them. Peggy, in *Hurricane!*, gets new glasses. She needs them to see, but she is scared that she will not look good in them. Her mother and father tell her that is not true, but Peggy will not put them on. In this story, a scary something will show Peggy how special her glasses can be.

# HURRICANE!

Michael Dayton

"I don't like them," Peggy said.

"I like them," said her mother. "You look cute in them."

"Cute?" said Peggy. "That does it." She put her new glasses down.

"Look out!" her mother said. "You might scratch them."

"I don't care if I scratch them," Peggy said. "I don't want to use them."

"Peggy, you have needed glasses for a long time," her mother said.

Peggy's father came into the house. "The radio says a hurricane is coming," he said. "I need to get my boat from Little Jack's place. I will go to the fish store and see Little Jack. We can ride out to his house in his boat. Peggy, you may come if you like."

"I will go to the store for some food," said Peggy's mother. "Then we should be ready to weather the hurricane. Peggy, put your glasses on."

Peggy put her glasses on and left the house with her father. It was raining, and the wind blew black and blue clouds through the sky.

At the fish store, Peggy and her
father saw Little Jack on his boat. Peggy
liked Little Jack because he could make
her laugh. He looked up and saw Peggy.
"Do I know you?" he asked with a smile.
"You look like a girl called Peggy that
I know, but Peggy does not have glasses."

Peggy put her glasses away. "They make me look funny," she said.

"Around this place we need people who look funny," Little Jack said. "I don't want to look funny all alone."

"Little Jack," said Peggy's father, "we need a ride to your house. I want to get my boat."

"I will be happy to take you with me," Little Jack said. "I have to take my boat home. This is not the place to keep a boat in a storm. Jump on."

"We will have to move fast," said Peggy's father. "I don't want to be out in a boat in the hurricane."

"It will be all right," said Little Jack. "The last weather forecast on the radio said the hurricane was not coming right away. We have time." Little Jack turned the boat around. The boat moved slowly into the wind.

The boat moved into the bay. The wind began to blow and the rain came down. Water blew into the boat.

"Keep an eye out," Little Jack said to Peggy. "In this storm we could run over a tree in the water."

Peggy looked around, and she saw that something was in the water. She needed her glasses to see what it was. When she put them on, she screamed, "Little Jack! Over there! A boat is turned over! A man is in the water!"

"Get the rope!" called Little Jack.

Peggy had the rope to the man on her first try. Slowly the man swam over to them. Peggy and her father helped the man get into the boat. "Are you all right?" Peggy asked.

"I have a scratch or two and I am wet and cold, but I am all right," the man said.

"Peggy, if it weren't for you, we might not have seen this man," her father said.

"Now will you say you look funny in your glasses?" asked Little Jack.

"I don't know if I look funny or not," said Peggy with a laugh, "but my glasses will be with me from now on!"

## Questions

Read and think.
1. Why didn't Peggy like her new glasses?
2. What did help Peggy see what was in the water?
3. Why did Peggy say that her glasses will be with her from now on?

# STORM

In a storm,
the wind talks
with its mouth wide open.
It yells around corners
with its eyes shut.
It bumps into itself
and falls over a roof
and whispers
OH . . . Oh . . . oh . . .

*Adrien Stoutenberg*

# PREPARING FOR READING

## Learning Vocabulary

Listen.

spray

Read.

1. A hurricane may come in the <u>spring</u> or the <u>summer</u>.
2. The <u>pilot</u> of an airplane may fly into the hurricane.
3. He will fly on a <u>line</u> from the bay to the huge black clouds.
4. The <u>stars</u> were blinking in the night sky when the pilot flew away.

spring     summer     pilot
line       stars

## Developing Background

Read and talk.

### A Hurricane Forecast

In the last story, *Hurricane!*, Peggy and her father had to get their boat home because of a hurricane. What is a hurricane? Can weather forecasters tell when a hurricane will be roaring on to the land from the ocean? Will a hurricane come in spring or summer? Look at the pictures from weather satellites of a hurricane over the ocean. You can see the huge clouds. In *The Eye of the Storm*, you will read of a man who helps forecast a hurricane.

# THE EYE OF THE STORM

*Michael Dayton*

Lowell Genzlinger rides up to his airplane and looks at the stars in the sky. Lowell should be sleeping at this time of night, but there is little time for sleep now. On this hot spring night, the weather forecast is not good. A hurricane may be coming on to the land.

Now this airplane pilot must go to work. It is time for Lowell to fly into the eye of the storm.

Not many people can fly an airplane through a big storm. But that is what Lowell Genzlinger can do. He is a pilot who looks for a hurricane. He can let people know when a hurricane might be coming.

A hurricane is a huge storm with a big eye. There is a strong wind around this eye. But in the eye of a hurricane, the air is quiet.

A hurricane may grow when the air and the water are hot. Some come in the spring. Many come in the summer and fall.

A hurricane is very strong. The wind of a hurricane can snap a tree in two or turn over a big boat. There may be a flood with a hurricane. Last summer, Lowell saw a hurricane flood a city in one hour.

On this night, pictures from satellites in the sky show some strange clouds over the ocean. Could they be a hurricane? Lowell is asked to pilot his plane through the clouds.

Lowell looks at his map. He sees where the eye of the hurricane should be. He will fly in a line to the clouds.

For a pilot, flying into a storm is scary. Flying into a hurricane at night is very scary. How big will the storm be? How strong will the wind be?

At first, Lowell can see the stars in the sky. Then, slowly, black clouds move around his plane. He can not see at all. The wind is roaring now.

Lowell must get to the eye of this hurricane. He calls to land on his radio. "I can't fly in a line through this storm. The wind is too strong. I have to fly left, into the wind to get to the eye."

All around Lowell's plane, the storm is roaring with lightning and thunder. The wind and rain rock the plane. Will Lowell make it through this storm?

Then the wind and the rain stop. All around his plane, Lowell can see a line of clouds where the lightning and thunder are. But where he is now, the air is quiet. He is in the eye of a hurricane!

Lowell looks up. There is not a cloud in the sky, and he can see the stars. On his radio, he calls to people on land. "The storm will move in a line out over the ocean," he says.

It was a long night. For now, Lowell's lifesaving work is over. He can fly home and get some sleep.

This may be the last hurricane of the spring. But if a hurricane should come this summer or fall, Lowell will be ready. He will jump into his plane and fly into the eye of the storm.

## Questions

Read and think.

1. Why does Lowell fly in his airplane to look for a hurricane?
2. What things can the wind of a hurricane do?
3. How could the work that Lowell does be a big help to you and your family?

# PREPARING FOR READING

## Learning Vocabulary

Listen.

letter

let • ter

thunder     summer     instrument

Read.

1. How can you <u>measure</u> the rain with your own instrument?
2. You will need a <u>ruler</u> and a can.
3. Now you can write a <u>report</u> on how to measure rain.

measure     ruler     report

## Developing Background

Read and talk.

### Your Own Weather Forecast

The TV or radio can tell you a weather report and forecast for the next day. You can write a weather report, too. *A Weather Report* will tell you what to do. You will need to make an instrument called a rain gauge. You will need to make a wind gauge and a weather vane, too. Read and see why you need these things to make your own weather report.

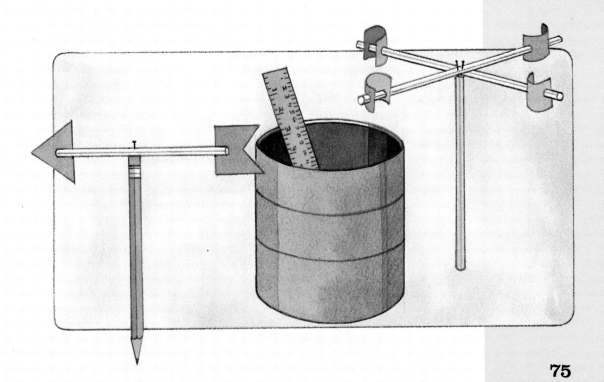

# A WEATHER REPORT

*Marlyn Mangus*

You know many of the things that make up the weather. You know how weather forecasters tell what the weather is like. You can tell what the weather is like, too. If you go out, you know if it is hot or cold. You know if it is raining. You can tell if the wind is strong. You can see if there are clouds in the sky.

You may want to measure the things that make up the weather. Then you can make a weather report.

Did it rain? You may want to know how much rain came down. A rain gauge will tell you.

You can make your own rain gauge with a can and a ruler. Use a ruler that will show both inches and centimeters.

Put your rain gauge out in the rain. When the rain is over, measure the water in the can with the ruler. You can measure the water in inches and centimeters.

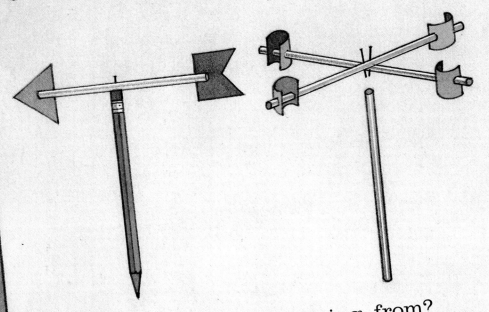

Where is the wind coming from? You can make a weather vane that will tell you. When the wind is blowing, your weather vane points into the wind. You can tell where the wind is coming from.

Is the wind blowing strong? You can make a wind gauge that will help tell you. When the wind is strong, your wind gauge will turn very fast. When there is little wind, it will move slowly. The pictures show you how to make these weather instruments.

Now you are ready to make your weather report. Each day you can write down what you see when you go out. You can write down what you measure with each instrument. Your report may look like this:

## WEATHER REPORT

From _____ to _____, 19__   Name: _____

| Day | Was it hot or cold? | Were there clouds or sun? | What was the wind like? | Did it rain? How much? |
|-----|---------------------|---------------------------|-------------------------|------------------------|
| 1 | warm | clouds | strong wind from north | yes, ⅜ inch (1 centimeter) |
| 2 | | | | |
| 3 | | | | |
| 4 | | | | |
| 5 | | | | |
| | | | | |

How many days did you report the weather all together? _____

How many days were cold? _____

How many days were hot? _____

How many days was there sun? _____

How many days were there clouds? _____

How many days was there a strong wind? _____

How many days was it raining? _____

How much did it rain all together?

How long did you keep your weather report? You can now tell what the weather was like for all the time of your report.

# Questions

Read and think.

1. What can you use to make your own rain gauge?
2. What instrument can tell you where the wind is coming from?
3. What instrument can tell you how strong the wind is?

# PREPARING FOR READING

## Learning Vocabulary

Listen.

swan

Read.

1. A warm <u>sweater</u> is special on a cold day in <u>winter</u>.
2. The <u>snow</u> can make your <u>feet</u> very cold, too.
3. The girl <u>wrote</u> in the snow.

sweater    winter    snow
feet    wrote

## Developing Background

Read and talk.

### First Snow

Look at the snow! Every winter people like to play in the first snow. Some like to walk in it. The wind may blow the snow all around you in the cold air. Some people like to make the first snowman of the winter. Some people put out food for the birds in the snow. In *A Walk in the Snow*, Eric does not like snow, but his sister does. Do you like to play in the snow?

# A Walk In The Snow

*Gibbs Davis*

"Come on, Eric," Cathy said to her brother. She walked through the falling snow.

Eric looked lost in his big new winter sweater. "I don't like this snow," he said. "Why does Grandma have to live up north like this? She should live where it doesn't snow, like us."

"Grandma should live where she wishes," said Cathy. She wrote something in the snow—

GRANDMA'S HOUSE

"I want to go in," said Eric. "Isn't the 'Funny Duck Show' on TV now?" Cathy walked on. "Wait for me!" called Eric, running after her.

"It helps to pick your feet up high," Cathy said. When she spoke, the cold air turned into a little cloud. Eric walked after Cathy, his feet falling through the high winter snow with each step. Walking in the snow was quiet, like walking in sneakers.

Cathy came to a stop under some big trees. "This is the place," she said.

"For what?" asked Eric.

Cathy wrote in the snow—

A WINTER PICNIC

"We need picnic food," said Eric. "Like a hot dog or something to drink. I know a good place at home for a picnic. We could go swimming there."

"I will make you my winter special," said Cathy. "One snow dog coming up."

Eric said, laughing, "A snow dog! I must write and tell Sam. He can't make a snow dog."

"Ready to go?" asked Cathy.

"I can't," Eric said. "My feet are so cold they can't move." Cathy wrote—

TRY

"Time to make a snowman," Cathy said. She began to make a big ball of snow.

"If I help you, my new winter sweater will get all wet," said Eric.

"Then keep an eye out for the snow lion," said Cathy.

"What snow lion?" asked Eric.

"The one with huge feet who likes to step on small people like you." Eric looked into the woods. "But I know what will keep it away," Cathy said.

"What?" asked Eric.

Cathy wrote—

A SNOWMAN

Eric helped Cathy make the last ball
of snow. "He's pretty scary, isn't he?"
said Eric, looking at the huge snowman.
He had sneakers for feet, a sweater, and
a rock for each eye.

"Something is missing," said Cathy,
"like glasses."

"Why does a snowman need glasses?"
asked Eric. "He can't read."

"Something is missing," said Cathy. "What is it?" Eric didn't know. They looked at the snowman a long time. Then Cathy wrote—

A SMILE

They picked up some small rocks from under the snow and put them on the snowman for a smile.

"Cathy! Eric! Time to eat!" It was Grandma. Eric looked at her house. It looked pretty under the falling snow. He looked at their picnic place under the trees and at the snowman with the funny smile.

"Come on," said Cathy.

"Coming," said Eric. But first he had something to do. He wrote in the snow—

I LIKE SNOW

## Questions

Read and think.

1. Why did Eric and Cathy go where it was cold?
2. What food did Cathy say she could make?
3. What did Cathy say they should do to keep the snow lion away?
4. Why did Eric write, "I like snow"?

# Winter Walk

I like days in winter
when paths are packed with snow
and feet make creaky footsteps
wherever footsteps go,
            and
I like days in winter
when snow lies soft and deep
and footsteps go so quietly
you'd think they were asleep.

*Aileen Fisher*

# PREPARING FOR READING

## Learning Vocabulary

Listen.

swan

Read.

1. The woman <u>sweeps</u> the snow from the <u>ice</u>.
2. Now we can go <u>skating</u>.
3. Some people like to ride on a <u>sled</u> or go <u>skiing</u> in the winter.
4. Winter is a time for <u>fun</u>.

sweeps    ice     skating
sled       skiing  fun

## Developing Background

Read and talk.

### Things to Do

Spring, summer, fall, and winter all have special things to do for fun. Spring is a good time to go fishing. Swimming is something many people like to do in the summer. Fall sweeps in, and it is time to report to school and see good friends. What can one do for fun in the winter? The story, *Winter Fun*, will tell you some of the things. What winter fun things do you like?

# WINTER FUN

*Alice Boynton*

It is winter. Children can't wait for the first snow. Then one day they get their wish. Snow is falling!

In the country and in the city, girls and boys are rushing out to play. Rita and José take their sled to the park. Some children make their own sled. They get a funny ride. Three people can ride on a very long sled. Their dog likes to get on, too.

A team can ride on one long sled and race. Their sled can go very fast on the snow and ice. There they go! If you look away, you may miss them go by.

If the weather is very cold, there may be ice for skating. Some people like to go ice skating. People can do many things on ice. Some race, some turn, some dance, and some fall!

A special truck can go on the ice. The truck helps people go skating because it sweeps the ice. After the truck sweeps, the children rush out to have fun on the ice.

This family likes to go skiing in the winter. They ride to the top and look out over the country. John sees a farm and a house, but they look very small because he is up so high.

Mother and Father are skiing down first, Bibi is next, and John is last. Each one sweeps down on the snow. The trees are rushing by. Bibi says skiing is fun because it is like flying.

What is in the picture? It is a strange
something! The boys and girls wanted
to make something special out of snow,
and they did. Can you tell what it is?

The children began with a big snowball. They had to work for a long time to make the snowball look like this. Then they put water on the snow, and it turned to ice. The children looked at their work, and they were happy with it.

There are so many things to do in the winter. Winter can be fun!

# Questions

Read and think.

1. What do many children wish for in winter?
2. What things do people do in the winter?
3. How can a truck help people who are ice skating?
4. How did the children make a huge something out of snow?

# PREPARING FOR READING

## Learning Vocabulary

Listen.

letter

let • ter

store  blanket  winter

Read.

1. The <u>busy</u> <u>ant</u> liked to work.
2. The <u>grasshopper</u> didn't like to work.
3. The grasshopper liked <u>singing</u>, but the ant did not.

busy   ant

grasshopper  singing

## Developing Background

Read and talk.

### A Fable

Do you like to work or play? In *The Ant and the Grasshopper*, the grasshopper does not work, but does play all the time. The ant does not play, but does work all the time. The grasshopper will not get ready for winter. The ant works in the spring and the summer to be ready for the winter. This story is called a *fable*. A fable is a little story that teaches something. What does the fable teach you?

# The Ant and the Grasshopper

*retold by Dorothy Van Woerkom*

One warm spring day a grasshopper walked through the park. She was singing, "It is spring and the park is warm! The park is a happy place to be."

Then she saw an ant sweeping out her house. "You look busy," the grasshopper said. "Why are you sweeping out your house?"

The ant said, "I want to make a place to store food for the winter."

"Winter!" said the grasshopper, laughing. "But this is spring, and spring is a time for singing."

"Spring is a time to be busy," said the ant. "It is a time to get food and put it away for the winter."

Then the grasshopper said, "If you like to work, don't let me stop you!" She walked away singing, "It is spring and the park is warm! The park is a happy place to be."

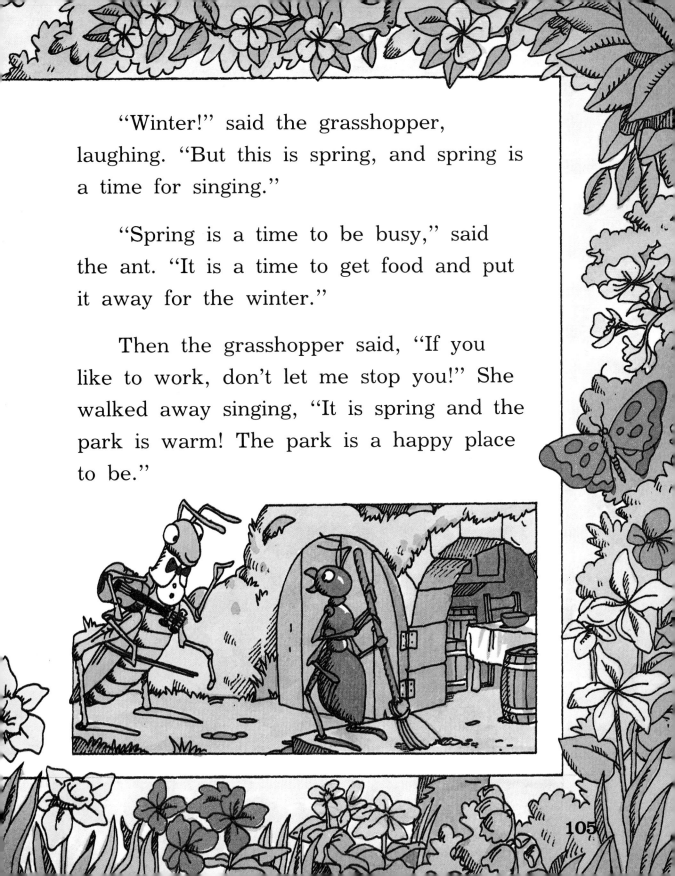

Summer came, and with it came the hot weather. The grasshopper liked the hot weather. She danced through the park singing, "It is summer and the park is green! The park is a happy place to be."

Then she saw the ant come home with some food. The ant put the food in her house. "You look busy," the grasshopper said. "Is that food for the winter?"

"It is," said the ant. "I will eat some of it now and put some away."

"But this is summer!" the grasshopper said. "This is a time to dance. You were busy all spring. Come away now and dance with me."

"This is not a time to dance," said the ant. "This is a time to be busy. I must store some food for the long cold winter. Grasshopper, you must get ready for the winter, too. Now is the time to do it. If you don't have food, you will not like the winter!"

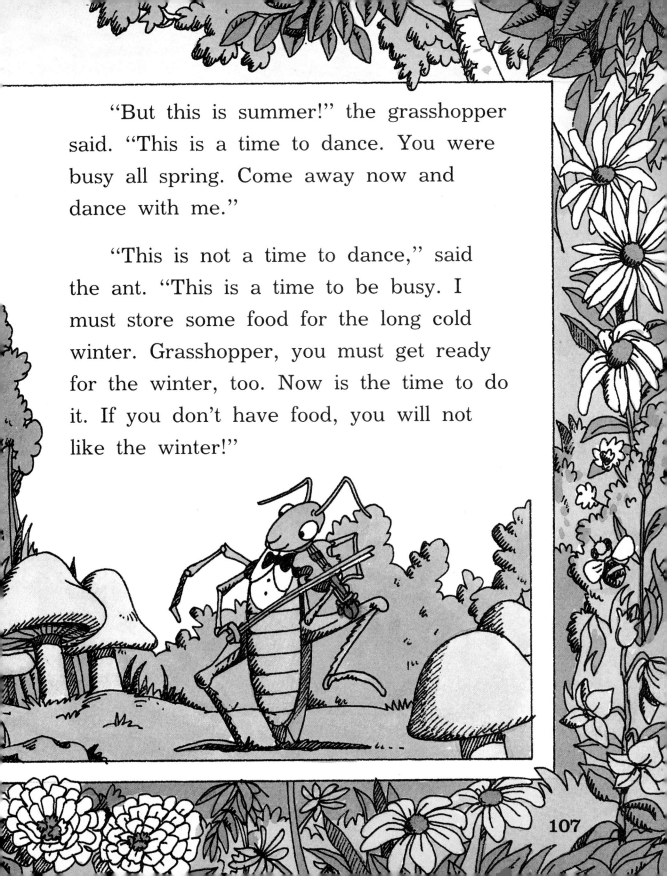

But the grasshopper said, "You are not much fun, Ant, but don't let me stop you!" She walked away singing, "It is summer and the park is green! The park is a happy place to be."

Fall came, and with it came the cold wind. The wind blew, and rain was falling. The park was cold, and wet, and brown. The grasshopper sang, "It is fall and the park is wet! My house is a happy place to be."

After the rain, she walked through the park, where she saw the ant spread some food out on the step of her house. "The rain wet some of my food," said the ant. "I have to put it out in the air. There is a little time left for you to get ready for the winter, Grasshopper. You should store some food, too."

"You can't know what it is like to dance and have fun, because you are busy all the time," said the grasshopper. "But don't let me stop you!" She walked home singing, "It is fall and the park is wet! My house is a happy place to be."

Winter came, and with it came the snow. The park was very cold now. "I need some food!" said the grasshopper. She called to the ant, "Will you let me have some of your food?"

But the ant said, "You could have had food of your own, Grasshopper. But you wanted to dance and play all the time. Now it is my turn to play, and it is your turn to work." So the grasshopper walked away to look for something to eat.

Now the ant was singing, and this is what she sang: "I was busy all spring when the grasshopper played. I was busy all summer and fall. Now it is winter and I have my food. The park is a happy place to be!"

# Questions

Read and think.

1. Who played all the time and did not get ready for winter?

2. What did the ant do to get ready for winter?

3. Why didn't the ant let the grasshopper have some of her food?

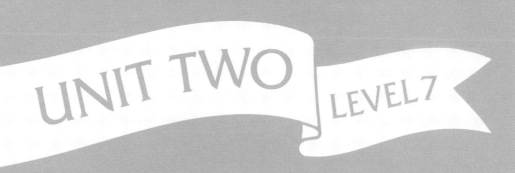

# UNIT TWO — LEVEL 7

# OUT AND ABOUT

# PREPARING FOR READING

## Learning Vocabulary

Listen.

tent

Read.

1.  The girls <u>went</u> to an <u>island</u> for a picnic.
2.  Each one had <u>lunch</u> in a <u>bag</u>.
3.  What did they see <u>stuck</u> by a rock on the island?

went    island    lunch    bag    stuck

114

## Developing Background

Read and talk.

### Day Camp

Many children like to go to camp. Some go away from home to camp. Some go to day camp. In day camp you come home every night. At day camp you can take trips to see special things. You can take your lunch in a bag and go on a picnic. You can go swimming or paint pictures. In *Island Friends*, some children in a day camp go to a small island in the city for a picnic.

# ISLAND FRIENDS

*Susan J. Shillcock*

At last the day had come for the children at the day camp to take their special trip. They walked with the teacher through the woods.

They had come to a very special park for a picnic. This park was in the city, but it was not like the city at all. This park was on an island. The city noise was not in this park. There was a quiet kind of noise that came from the birds singing in the trees, and the water all around.

Jane went over to sit by the water with her lunch bag. She missed her friend Nan. Nan had moved away, and Jane didn't know if she could make a new friend. She looked around. A bird was flying through the trees, and a rabbit was eating its lunch over by the rocks. A grasshopper was right next to her foot.

Then Jane saw a rock move. Now what could that be? Rocks don't move! Then she began to smile when she saw what it was. It was not a rock after all. It was a turtle!

Now Jane could see that the turtle was turned over on its shell. It was stuck by two rocks next to the water. The turtle needed help, but what could she do?

Jane looked around and saw that her teacher was very busy with some of the children over by the trees. She looked down at her new sneakers and then at the cold water. She wanted to get to the turtle right away, but she didn't want to get her new sneakers all wet.

Then Jane saw how she could help the turtle, but she needed a friend to help her. She looked around. Then she saw Anita, who was looking into her lunch bag.

"Anita!" called Jane. "Will you come and help me? I want to show you something by the water."

Anita came over to Jane. "What is it? What do you see?" she asked.

"Look at the place by the rocks," said Jane. "Do you see the turtle there? It is stuck, and I want you to help me. May I use your lunch bag?"

"You may have my lunch," said Anita, "but how will that help the turtle?"

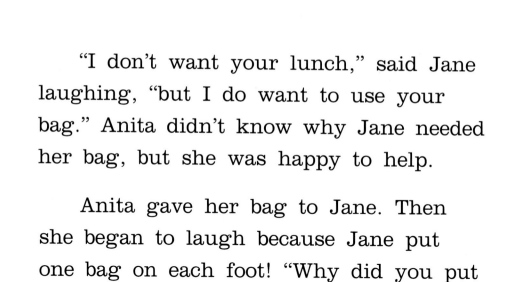

"I don't want your lunch," said Jane laughing, "but I do want to use your bag." Anita didn't know why Jane needed her bag, but she was happy to help.

Anita gave her bag to Jane. Then she began to laugh because Jane put one bag on each foot! "Why did you put them on your feet?" asked Anita. "It looks funny."

"Because now my sneakers can't get wet when I step in the water. Wait and see," Jane said. She went slowly through the cold water over to the place where the turtle was stuck on its shell. She could see that it was a box turtle. She spoke to the turtle, "Don't be scared, I will help you." She did not pick the turtle up. She slowly turned it over with one foot. "Now that you are not stuck you can go home," she said.

Jane turned and called to Anita, "I put the turtle on its feet, and it went into the woods. First you helped me, and then I helped the turtle!"

"And your sneakers are not wet," said Anita.

"My sneakers are not wet, but your lunch bag is all wet. You can't use it for your lunch now," said Jane.

"I know, but I don't need it. We can have lunch together now," Anita said.

"I like this island," said Anita after lunch. "I wish we could take a trip like this every day with the day camp, don't you?"

"I wish we could," Jane said. "My father likes to walk with me in the park. Someday he may like to take me to this island. If he does, could you come too?"

"I hope so," said Anita.

"I am so happy to have a new friend!" said Jane.

"You have *two* new friends," said Anita, laughing. "Me and the turtle!"

# Questions

Read and think.
1. What did Jane see stuck in the water?
2. What did Anita let Jane have to help the turtle?
3. How did Jane help the turtle?
4. Why didn't Jane want to walk in the water?

# THE TURTLE

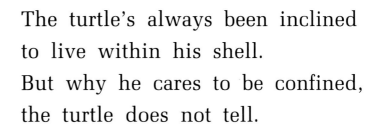

The turtle's always been inclined
to live within his shell.
But why he cares to be confined,
the turtle does not tell.

The turtle's always satisfied
to slowly creep and crawl,
and never wanders far outside
his living room or hall.

So if you wish to visit him
in his domestic dome,
just knock politely on his shell,
you'll find the turtle home.

*Jack Prelutsky*

# PREPARING FOR READING

## Learning Vocabulary

Listen.

| bird | birds |
| fox | foxes |
| child | children |

Read.

1. Many animals live on the island.
2. Remember to walk with care.
3. You can take a trail into the swamp.
4. It is fun to be here on the island.

animals    remember    trail
swamp    here

## Developing Background

Read and talk.

### An Island

What is an island? An island is land with water all around it. An island can be little or big. An island may be in a bay or in the ocean. People can live on an island or birds and animals can live on it alone. *Island in the City* is a story of a little island in the Potomac River in Washington, D.C. Look at the picture of things in Washington, D.C. Your teacher will help you look for this special city on a map of the United States.

127

# ISLAND IN THE CITY

### VIRGINIA ARNOLD

Washington, D.C., is a big, busy city. Many people come to see Washington, D.C., but many of them miss a very special park right in the city. They drive right by it and do not know it is here.

This park is on an island. The park is called Theodore Roosevelt Island, and it is in the Potomac River. The Potomac River runs by the city of Washington, D.C.

Theodore Roosevelt was a president of the United States. We remember him because he was a president who liked the land, water, woods, and animals. We remember Theodore Roosevelt, too, because he began many parks in the United States. Then and now, the parks keep the land for all the people to use.

Many people wanted to make a special park for Theodore Roosevelt. Theodore Roosevelt Island is that park.

Here is Theodore Roosevelt on his island. Here you can read some things he said when he was President of the United States.

Theodore Roosevelt Island is a quiet place in a busy city. People may come for a walk or a run around the island. Small animals and birds make their home here.

This map can show you each trail you can use on the island. The Woods Trail and the Swamp Trail go around the island. The Upland Trail will take you to the high place on the island. Remember to read the map so that you don't get lost on the island.

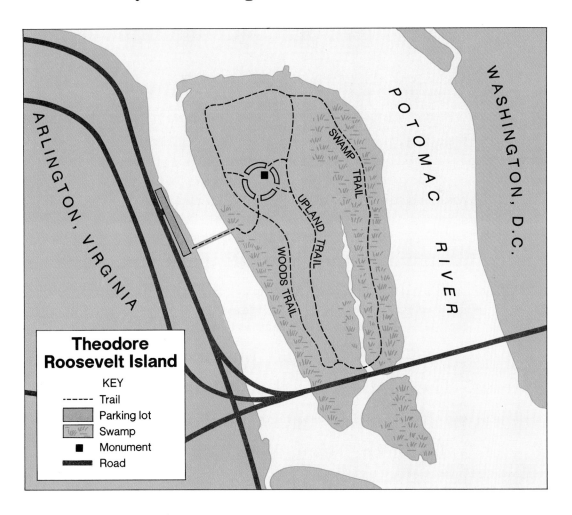

Theodore Roosevelt Island

KEY

- - - - - Trail
Parking lot
Swamp
■ Monument
Road

ARLINGTON, VIRGINIA

WASHINGTON, D.C.

POTOMAC RIVER

SWAMP TRAIL

UPLAND TRAIL

WOODS TRAIL

When you come into the park, the Woods Trail is the first trail you will see. On this trail, you will see many birds, some small animals, and big and small trees. The Upland Trail will take you through the island, not around it. When you walk on this trail, you can see a little of the city through the trees.

On the Swamp Trail, you will walk by the Potomac River. Many small animals and birds live in the water of the swamp and on the river, too. Don't take this trail when it is raining, because it is too wet.

Theodore Roosevelt Island is a very special place. It is a quiet park in a busy city.

# Questions

Read and think.

1. In what big city is Theodore Roosevelt Island?
2. Why did people want to make a special park for Theodore Roosevelt?
3. When you come into the park, what is the first trail you will see?

# PREPARING FOR READING

## Learning Vocabulary

Listen.

boy          points

Read.

1. Fred's music gave his friends much <u>joy</u>.
2. His friends liked to <u>hear</u> his <u>songs</u>.
3. Fred jumped on a <u>train</u> for the city.
4. Singing in all the city noise was <u>hard</u> for <u>him</u>.

joy      hear    songs
train    hard    him

## Developing Background
Read and talk.

### Country Music

People get joy from music. Country music is one kind of music people like to hear. It can make one happy or sad. Country songs may tell of people who live in the country. They may tell of country people who live in the city but want to go home to the country. Country songs may tell a story of animals or the big woods. In *Fred and Friends*, you will read of Fred the Grasshopper and his country music.

# FRED AND FRIENDS

VIRGINIA A. ARNOLD

Fred the Grasshopper had a small home in the country. He liked his home, and he liked his friends. But Fred's joy was his music. Fred liked country music. He liked singing sad songs and happy songs. He liked to write country songs, too. Fred's music gave much joy to his friends in the country. Many of them said to him, "Fred, you should go to the city and make country music for city people. You could be a star."

Fred said, "I might like that, but will city people like country music?"

One day Fred said, "I will go to the city, and I will go by train." Fred went down to the train. He jumped on, and away he went.

"Remember us when you are a star," his friends called to him.

"I will," Fred said.

Later that night the train came into the city. Fred jumped out of the train and looked around. "What noise!" he said. "What rushing around! It is hard to move around here. I don't want people to step on me." Right then a truck came roaring by, and Fred jumped to get away. SPLAT! Right into some water went Fred. "Help!" he screamed. "I can't swim!"

Then something right next to him said, "I will help you. Jump on!" A big waterbug was swimming by. Fred jumped up and away they swam. The waterbug said, "I am Willie Waterbug. I see this is your first time in the city. Why not come home with me?"

"I will be happy to," said Fred.

Later at Willie's house, Fred said, "I came to the city to play my country music for city people. I want them to like it."

"I play a little country, too," said Willie. "Let us try to play some music together." And they did.

Willie said, "You are very good, but it will be hard to be a star in the city. You may wish you had not moved here."

"I can work hard, but I can't do it alone," said Fred. "I don't want to be a star if I don't have friends. I need three friends to help me make my music."

Willie said, "I know Amanda Ant. She can make a drum jump. Mike Fly can make some beautiful music. I will get both of them together with us."

"Good," said Fred.

In very little time, Fred and his friends were singing and playing his country songs all over the city.

It was very hard to play in the city. With all the rushing and roaring, people couldn't hear something right next to them. How could they hear Fred's music? "What can we do?" asked Fred. Amanda and Mike looked very sad, and so did Fred.

"Wait," said Willie. "There is an island right here in the city. It is quiet, and people can hear us."

"If they can hear us," said Mike, "I know they will like us."

"And," said Amanda, "if they like us, I know we will be stars."

"I will like it if they can hear us," said Fred. "Stars or not."

They did go to the quiet little island. Fred and his friends began to play their country songs, and people could hear them there. Their country music gave the city people much joy, and Amanda was right. Now they are called *Fred and Friends*, and they are stars of country music.

Fred did remember his friends in the country. When he went to see them, they all said, "Come home, Fred."

Fred said, "Now my home is in the city. I will come to see you, but I like my city island." Fred is there to this day. Every day and night you can hear *Fred and Friends* playing country music for city people.

## Questions

Read and think.
1. What did Fred the Grasshopper like to do?
2. Why was Fred sad when he first played his music for the people in the city?
3. Where did Willie say the friends should go to play their music?

# PREPARING FOR READING

## Learning Vocabulary

Listen.

b<u>oy</u>          p<u>oi</u>nts

Read.

1. A new boy came to <u>join</u> our school.
2. He had to <u>travel</u> a long time <u>before</u> he could get here.
3. He will live on my <u>street</u>.
4. The teacher said to him, "<u>Hello</u>! <u>Please</u> sit by Bobby."

join          travel          before
street          hello          please

## Developing Background

Read and talk.

### Soccer

What is a team game that might be played in each country? It's soccer. Soccer is played by many boys and girls in the United States, too. There may be a soccer team in your school. Soccer is played with a soccer ball. You must have strong legs and feet in soccer, for you must run fast in the game. What are some things you can and can't do with the ball in soccer? In *The New Boy*, who helps Bobby and his friends with their soccer game?

# THE NEW BOY

Johanna Hurwitz

One day, a new boy came to Green School. Mrs. Clark said, "This is Le Nam Cuong. Before he came to join us, he had his home in Vietnam. Cuong had to travel a long time to get to the United States. Now he will live on Spring Street and come to Green School."

All the boys and girls looked at Cuong. He did not look like them. He looked sad and a little scared, too.

"Cuong, we know how long you had to travel to get here," said Mrs. Clark. Cuong looked at Mrs. Clark, but he was very quiet. Mrs. Clark went on, "Cuong does know a little English, but we will need to help him. Cuong, we will try to make you happy that you came to join us."

Mrs. Clark looked at Bobby Andrews. "Cuong, this is Bobby Andrews. Please sit here next to him. Bobby can help you with your school work and your English. You both live on Spring Street."

"Hello Cuong," said Bobby.

Cuong said, "Hello," but he looked away.

It was before lunch so the boys and girls did some of their work. At first, they had to make a picture of their house. Then they each had to write a story to go with their picture.

Cuong looked at Bobby's pictures. He began making pictures, too. His pictures were of his house in Vietnam. But Cuong couldn't write a story in English. "Bobby, will you please help Cuong write his story?" asked Mrs. Clark.

Bobby said, "Before we write, Cuong, tell me where your home was. What was your street like?"

Cuong had pictures of a farm. "We left this farm to travel to your country," he said.

"That must be why you are sad," said Bobby. "There is not a farm here in the city, but you will like the city, too."

When it was time for lunch, Bobby began to walk fast. "Come with me," he said to Cuong. "I will show you where we can sit together. You will not be alone here. I will be your friend."

When lunch was over, the boys and
girls went out to play. Cuong was very
quiet, but he went out after Bobby.
Where Bobby went, Cuong went. Bobby
was happy, but he wanted Cuong to be
happy, too. "What do you like to play?"
he asked. Cuong didn't say.

The children began a game of soccer. "May I play this game?" asked Cuong. "I know soccer."

Bobby did not know how much Cuong had played soccer before in Vietnam. "You may join us," he said. "You will be on my team. Do what you can."

Cuong said, "I will try hard. I played soccer in Vietnam."

"Hello, Bobby," said one of the boys on Bobby's team. "Does Cuong know how to play? We don't want to be stuck with him if he's not making points."

"He can play," said Bobby, but
Bobby was a little scared. Did Cuong
know how to play soccer?

The game began. Bobby's team had
the ball. Then Cuong went running with
the ball. His feet flew. He could kick and
run. He could make points! The children
screamed, "Hurray! Hurray for Cuong!
You can play soccer. You should be on
the school soccer team!"

For the first time, Cuong gave a little smile. "I like soccer. We will play together?" he asked Bobby.

"We will play together," said Bobby.

Cuong asked, "You will help me read and write?"

"I will help you read and write if you will help me play soccer," said Bobby.

"I will help," said Cuong.

Bobby gave Cuong a big smile. "Can you play basketball, too? How do you like swimming?" Bobby went rushing on. "You will like skiing and skating, too."

Now Cuong had a big smile, too. "Wait," he said. "You go too fast. Please go slowly."

Bobby said, "You are right. We don't need to go so fast. This is home for you now. Come on, it is time to go in."

Cuong said, "Soccer, a new friend, and a home. All in one day!"

# Questions

Read and think.
1. Where did Cuong come from?
2. Who did Cuong sit next to in school?
3. What did the teacher want Bobby to do?
4. Why did Cuong smile when he played soccer?

# WRITING ACTIVITY

## WRITE A LETTER

### Prewrite

In *The New Boy*, Cuong gets a new friend, a new school, and gets to play soccer all in one day. What if you were in Green School that day?

You might write a letter to a friend. You will want to tell your friend of Cuong's first day and the soccer game. What will you tell first? Then what will you tell? What sentences will you write for your letter?

Your letter will look like this.

March __, 19__

Dear _____ ,
   A new boy came to my school.

Your friend,

_____

## Write

1. Write your letter on your paper.
2. Your first sentence might be like the one in the letter on page 154.
3. Now write sentences that tell of Cuong's first day at Green School.
4. Use your Glossary for help with words.

## Revise

Read your letter. Do your sentences tell what Cuong did on his first day? Did you use words like *first*, *next*, and *last*? If not, try to use them now.

Read with your teacher.

1. Did you capitalize the names of people?
2. Did you write each part of the letter correctly?

# PREPARING FOR READING

## Learning Vocabulary

Listen.

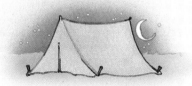

tent

 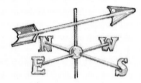 

Read.

1. The family will go on an <u>important</u> trip.

2. They want to <u>learn</u> <u>about</u> places they will see before they go.

3. It is <u>as</u> important to know what you will see as it is to know how to get there.

4. The woman at the travel store will use her <u>computer</u> to help them with the trip.

important      learn           about

as             computer

## Developing Background

Read and talk.

### A Travel Store

Do you like to take trips? Then you will like to go to a travel store. At the store, you may tell a man where you want to go and what you want to see. You tell him if you want to go by plane, train, bus, boat, or car. He will use his computer to pick the right trip for you. You will get a map and a book about your trip. In *Going to England*, Maggie's family will go to a travel store for help with their trip.

GOING TO ENGLAND

Marlyn Mangus

Maggie was very happy when she began to learn about England in school. England was an important place to Maggie. Her mother and father came from England. She and her family were going to take a trip there. Maggie wanted to learn as much as she could about the country before she went.

Maggie began to learn new things by talking with her mother and father. She asked them to tell her the things they could remember about what it was like to grow up in England. They gave Maggie a book about England. The book had pictures of many English people and places. Maggie looked at TV, too, to learn about England.

Because of Maggie's family and because of her trip, Maggie's teacher asked her to tell the children some special things about England. Here are some of the important things Maggie wrote down to tell at school. Here, too, are some of the pictures Maggie had to show the children.

England is an island country. You must fly over the ocean to get there from the United States.

The people in England use English, as we do in the United States. But they do not say all things as we do. In England, TV is called "telly." A truck is called a "lorry."

Here is a picture of an English bus and an English car. The bus is very high, and the car is very small. Look how the English drive. Do you see something strange?

In the United States we have a president. In England they have a queen. The queen and her family own some castles and live in them. There are many castles in England. At one time castles were very important places.

The English have a game called cricket. Cricket is like a game we play. Do you know what game that is?

Now Maggie and her family were ready to take their trip. They went to see the woman at the travel store. The woman asked them where they wanted to go. She asked them when they wanted to go and how long they wanted to travel. The woman asked the family to tell her the important places they wanted to see.

The woman had a computer to help her with the trip. The computer could help the woman pick the plane that Maggie and her family were going to fly on. The woman at the travel store could use the computer to help Maggie and her family pick the places where they were going to eat and sleep.

Maggie said that the computer looked as if it might be fun to use.

At last the day came to go on the trip. Maggie was not on the plane very long before she went to sleep. Before long she was going to be in England! At last she was going to see all the people, places, and things she had read about. And she was going to learn many new things about England, too.

# Questions

Read and think.

1. Why did Maggie want to learn as much as she could about England?
2. What is strange about how the English drive?
3. How did the woman at the travel store help Maggie's family get ready for their trip?

# PREPARING FOR READING

## Learning Vocabulary

Listen.

bank

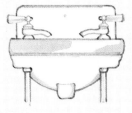

Read.

1. I wrote to <u>thank</u> my friend for her last letter.
2. She wrote to tell me about the <u>cows</u> on their new farm.
3. They use <u>machines</u> to <u>milk</u> the cows.
4. We milk <u>our</u> cows with machines, too.

thank     cows     machines

milk     our

## Developing Background

Read and talk.

### A Farm

A farm is very important for all of us. On a farm, people grow many kinds of food that we need to eat. A special kind of farm is a dairy farm. We get our milk from the cows at the dairy. The eggs we need come from a chicken farm. The story, *Friends Through the Mail*, will tell about a dairy farm in Wisconsin in the United States and a farm in Denmark. Your teacher will help you look for Wisconsin and Denmark on a map.

Anne lives on a farm in Wisconsin. Lars lives on a farm, too, but his farm is in a country called Denmark. Anne writes a letter to Lars. She wants to know about his family and his farm.

Lars writes a letter to Anne. Some pictures come with his letter. Anne likes to read the letter and look at the pictures. The letter and the pictures help her learn what Lars's family and farm are like.

March 3, 1988

Dear Anne,

Thank you for your letter. I will try to let you know some things about my family. My mother, my father, my little brother Peter, and I live on a farm. Our farm is in Denmark. Here is our house:

Our farm is a dairy farm. We have many cows. There is much to do every day on the farm. We all help but Peter. He is two, and he is too little to help.

I feed the cows with my father. We must see that they have water, too.

My mother and father both help milk the cows. They use machines. With the machines, they can milk many cows at one time. A gauge tells how much milk there is.

We must keep the milk cold. A gauge tells how cold the milk is.

A truck like the one in the picture will come to take the milk.

We eat many things that come from milk. Here are some of them:

Do you know which one I like very much?

I hope you will write to me. I want to know about your family and what your farm is like. Do you have a brother or a sister? Do you have a pet?

Your friend,
Lars.

Anne writes this letter to Lars:

March 15, 1988

Dear Lars,
Thank you for your letter, and thank you for the pictures. I have some pictures for you, too. Here is a picture of my house.

My brother is Peter, too. Isn't that funny? But he is not small like your brother Peter!

Our family is very much like your family. Our farm is like your farm, too. It is a dairy farm in a place in the United States called Wisconsin.

Peter wants to have a dairy farm of his own someday. He will need to learn many things about the cows and the farm. Here my father teaches Peter how to use the machines that milk the cows:

We all have work to do on the farm. My mother and I help care for the animals and feed them.

Peter and I are both in school. We ride the bus to get there. Every day our pets wait with us for the school bus to come. We have a cat and a dog.

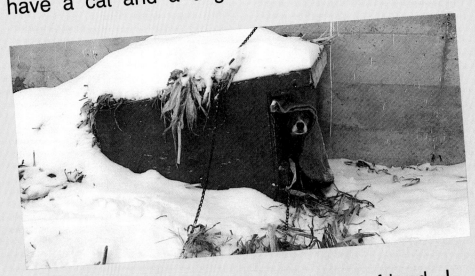

I am happy to have you for a friend. I hope to travel to Denmark to see you someday. Peter wants to come, too. We both hope you will come to Wisconsin someday to see us.

Your friend,
Anne

# Questions

Read and think.

1. Where is Lars's farm? Where is Anne's farm?
2. What do we get from a dairy farm?
3. How did Lars tell Anne about his farm?
4. What are some dairy things that you like to eat?

# PREPARING FOR READING

## Learning Vocabulary

Listen.

bat                    bats

wish                   wishes

family                 families

Read.

1. The school <u>buildings</u> on the island are not like my school at home.

2. <u>Soon</u> I hope I will like my school.

3. My father is making paints in the <u>plant</u> where he works.

4. My new friends <u>speak</u> a little English.

5. They did learn to say "<u>no</u>" in English.

buildings    soon    plant
speak        no

## Developing Background

Read and talk.

### Puerto Rico

Puerto Rico is an island. Look for Puerto Rico and the United States on a map. Puerto Rico is a beautiful island. The weather is warm both in the summer and the winter. There may be a little rain every day, but there will be some sun, too. The people of Puerto Rico speak Spanish. Many of them know some English, too. In *My New Home*, Irene and her family have moved to Puerto Rico. Irene does not speak Spanish. What will she do to make friends?

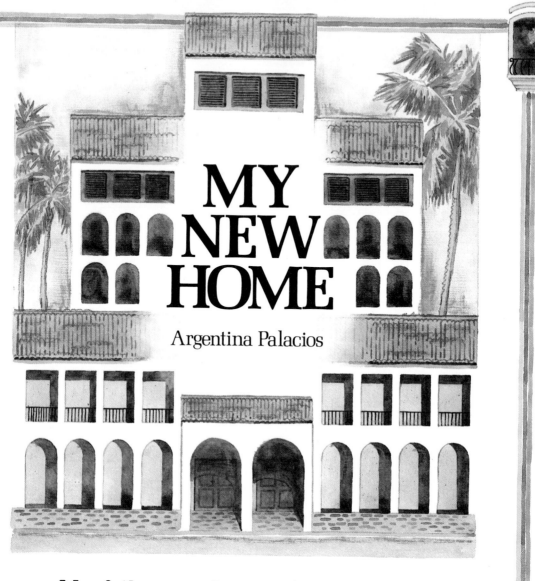

# MY NEW HOME

Argentina Palacios

My father works at a place where they make sneakers. They have a plant in the United States and one in Puerto Rico. My father did work at the plant in the United States, but now he works at the one in Puerto Rico.

I remember the day when my father came home from work and said we were going to move to Puerto Rico. I was sad and a little scared. I didn't say a thing, but my father was looking at me.

"Irene, don't you want to live in Puerto Rico?" he asked.

"Father," I said, "I will miss all my friends. And I don't know how to speak Spanish!"

My mother and father said many things to try to make me happy. "You will make new friends soon."

"Speaking Spanish is not hard. We know Spanish, and we will help you."

"Many people speak both Spanish and English."

"You can write to your friends. They might come to see you."

I looked at a map in a book and saw that Puerto Rico is an island. I read that the weather is good in Puerto Rico. I began to be happy about going there.

Soon the day came to go, and I was ready. We flew in a huge airplane. The first people we saw in Puerto Rico were some friends of my father. They drove us in their car to some big buildings. One of them was to be our new home. I liked the buildings and the busy street, too.

The next day my father drove to work with his friends because we didn't have a car. My mother was going to work at a computer plant. Her work began in three days, so she had time to show me around. First we had to see about a school for me. The next day I was in school.

At first, speaking Spanish was very hard for me. I was scared, but soon I saw that no one was laughing at me. I began to make friends very fast. My new friends liked to do all kinds of things. One wanted to be a ballet dancer, and one wanted to own a pet store. One liked basketball, and one liked skating. It was funny when they called me "Ee-ray-nay." That is how "Irene" is said in Spanish.

It was not hard to learn to speak Spanish with my friends. They helped me all the time. Then when my mother went to work, Rosa came to help me. Rosa is my babysitter and my Spanish teacher, too. And I am her English teacher!

One day we went to the swimming pool. I said to Rosa, "I like to swim." She said that "nadar" is how to say "to swim" in Spanish. When we were walking home we saw a dog running by the buildings. Rosa called it a "perro." I said to her, "Dog."

We now have a car, so my mother
and father can drive to work. When
there is no work and no school, the
family can go for a long drive in the
country. It is fun to live in a place
where it is warm all the time. I like
that very much, but sometimes I miss
the winter a little. You can't make a
snowman or a snowball in Puerto Rico!

One day, a letter came from Grandma and Grandpa. They wanted to come to see us. We were very happy, because we had not seen them for a long time.

The sky was blue and pretty when we went to pick them up. We had many things to show them on the drive home. They liked the hot weather and the green all around. When we were home, Grandma asked me, "Irene, are you sad that you came to live in Puerto Rico?"

"No, I am not," I said. "I am very happy here in my new home. And do you know what? I am called 'Ee-ray-nay!'"

"What do you know?" said Grandpa. "We have a Spanish-speaking girl now!"

# Questions

Read and think.

1. Why did Irene's family move to Puerto Rico?
2. Why didn't Irene want to move to Puerto Rico?
3. What kinds of things did Irene like in Puerto Rico?

# PREPARING FOR READING

## Learning Vocabulary

Listen.

wind

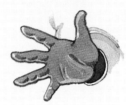

Read.

1. People <u>find</u> many kinds of buildings for homes.
2. There are many <u>different</u> kinds of buildings in the <u>world</u>.
3. Each of the buildings <u>has</u> a <u>roof</u>.
4. The roof may be <u>made</u> of many different things.

| find | different | world |
|------|-----------|-------|
| has  | roof      | made  |

184

## Developing Background

Read and talk.

## Homes

Many different kinds of buildings can be called homes. Look at the buildings in the picture. In the United States, we may live in homes that look like this. Homes can be in many different places, too. People have homes in the city and in the country. Some have homes on a boat. Some may live on an island. *Homes Around the World* is a story about different homes all around the world. Some of the homes are very different from the homes you know.

# Homes Around the World

### Marlyn Mangus

In our country, we have many kinds of homes. Some are alike and some are different. There are big homes and small homes, city homes and country homes. There are homes that are made for one family, and homes that are made for many.

Do you see a house that looks like your home?

All homes are much alike, because they are places where people live. In our homes we can keep out of the rain and wind. Our homes may help us keep warm in cold weather. Home is the place where we eat and sleep. It is where we do many things together with our family and friends.

Now let us look at some homes around the world. As you read and look at the pictures, try to find which homes are like homes in the United States. Try to find which homes are different, too.

Homes in Switzerland must be strong because of the wind and snow. Look at the roof on this house. The roof helps keep snow from falling around the house. Snow on the roof helps keep the house warm.

We find homes like this one on the warm island of Bermuda. This house has a special kind of roof. People in Bermuda store rain water falling on the roof to use as water to drink.

Many people in Mongolia live in a tent. It is not hard to take down this house when it is time to move. You might use a tent when you go camping.

In China, some people live in homes
that float. What kind of weather do they
have here? Can you see what kind of
roof the homes have ? What is it made of?

Here are some homes in a city in
Brazil. There is a place where the
children can play. There is a place where
people can swim. There are places where
people can sit out in warm weather. How
do the people get up and down?

You have seen that some homes around the world may be like your home. Some may be very different from your home. Homes around the world are made of different things. The kinds of homes people have may have to do with where they live and how they live.

## Questions

Read and think.
1. How does the roof on a home in Switzerland help the people who live there?
2. Why do many people in Mongolia live in a tent?
3. How are all homes alike?

# It's a Small World

It's a world of laughter,
  a world of tears;
It's a world of hopes and a world of fears.
There's so much that we share
  that it's time we're aware.
It's a small world after all.

*Chorus:* It's a small world after all,
  It's a small world after all.
  It's a small world after all,
  It's a small, small, world.

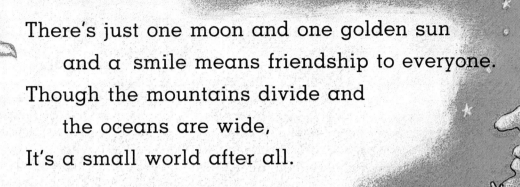

There's just one moon and one golden sun
    and a smile means friendship to everyone.
Though the mountains divide and
    the oceans are wide,
It's a small world after all.

*Chorus:* It's a small world after all,
        It's a small world after all.
        It's a small world after all,
        It's a small, small, world.

Richard Sherman and
Robert B. Sherman

# PREPARING FOR READING

## Learning Vocabulary

Listen.

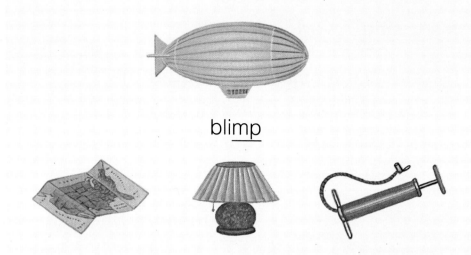

blimp

Read.

1. "Don't <u>bump</u> into me," calls Muffy to her friend.

2. "<u>Yes</u>, I need to keep my <u>balance</u> for this trick."

3. Muffy likes to do <u>exercises</u> for gymnastics.

4. <u>These</u> exercises look funny because Muffy lives in <u>space</u>.

| | | |
|---|---|---|
| bump | yes | balance |
| exercises | these | space |

## Developing Background

Read and talk.

### Gymnastics

Do you like to kick and jump and run? Then you will like gymnastics. Many boys and girls around the United States are on a gymnastics team at school. They learn to walk a balance beam and do many special exercises. Gymnastics is special to boys and girls around the world, too. *The Tryout* is a story about Tom, a boy who likes gymnastics and wants to be on a gymnastics team. What is different about Tom and his home?

# THE TRYOUT

Lorenca Consuelo Rosal

Home for Tom was a space station.
The space station was like an island city.
It was very busy. There was important
work to do at the station. People did
much of the work with computers. These
computers helped people learn of the
strange things that take place in space.

Tom's father was one of the weather
forecasters for the space station. He had
a weather satellite and computers to help
him forecast the weather. Tom's mother
needed computers to do her work, too. She
was making a new map of the many stars
that could be seen from the space station.

Tom was busy, too. He went to
school on the space station. He liked to
read about how people first began to
travel in the sky. There were pictures in
one book of a blimp and an airplane.
There were pictures of the first space
walk and the first satellite, too.

After school there was a park in which to play. There was a gym on the space station where Tom went to do his exercises. There were running machines, a balance beam, and a rope to work out with. There was a huge special box, too. In it Tom was lighter than air. Tom liked to float around. "I am a bird flying," he said.

One day the space circus came to the station. The space circus was run by the Rock People. Some of the Rock People were in the gym when Tom was. He was walking on the balance beam. "You are very good at these exercises," a Rock Man said to him. "You have good balance. You could be in our circus!"

"Thank you," Tom said with a smile. "I will soon try out for the gymnastics team."

Tom wanted so much to make the space station gymnastics team! Every day he did his exercises. At last it was time for the tryout. Tom looked a little scared. "Take your time," his mother said, "and remember, if you don't make the team this time, you will the next."

It was Tom's turn. With a big jump, he was up on the balance beam. But then Tom began to flounder. His foot began to slide. Down he came with a bump-bump-bump! His father and mother came rushing over. "Tom! Are you all right?" his father asked.

"How can I be all right when I will not make the team?" Tom said. "After all that hard work! I did these exercises over and over every day. Why did I

have to fall this time? I am through with gymnastics. I have had it!" Tom turned and walked away.

"But Tom . . ." said his father.

"Wait," said his mother. "He may need to be alone right now."

Tom wanted to run and hide. He wanted to get away as fast as he could. But how? He was on an island in space. "Yes, I know!" he said. "The circus. . . I will run away with the circus!"

Tom went to see the Rock People. "Hello little friend," said the Rock Man. "May I help you?"

"Yes, you may," said Tom. "I want to come with you and be in the circus."

With a smile the Rock Man asked, "Can you walk on a rope or fly through the air? Can you play circus music or train a bear to dance?"

"But you said I could be in the circus
because of my gymnastics!" said Tom.

The Rock Man could see Tom was sad.
"Yes, I did say that," said the Rock Man.
"Work very hard and do your exercises
every day. If your mother and father
will let you, you may be in the circus
every time we come to your space station."

Tom wanted to jump for joy. "Thank
you, thank you!" he said.

"So long, little friend," said the Rock Man.

Tom went home as fast as he could. He came roaring into the house.

"Mother, Father!" he called. "I will be in the circus! I have to go work out right away. I will be home to eat in an hour or two. See you then."

Tom's father looked at Tom's mother. "What in the world . . . "

"We should know by now," said Tom's mother with a smile, "that space is a strange place!"

# Questions

Read and think.
1. Where did Tom live?
2. What did the Rock Man say Tom could do if he did his exercises every day?
3. Why was Tom sad when he did not make the gymnastics team?

# PREPARING FOR READING

## Learning Vocabulary

Listen.

w<u>in</u>d

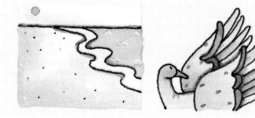

Read.

1. The boy <u>found</u> <u>presents</u> by his bed.
2. He <u>got</u> presents for his <u>birthday</u> from his family.
3. A friend <u>brings</u> him a present, too.
4. He will have a <u>cake</u> for his birthday <u>party</u>.

found      presents    got
birthday   brings      cake
party

## Developing Background

Read and talk.

### Your Birthday

A birthday is a very special day for you. What do you like to do on your birthday? Some people like a party with a big cake. Presents make a birthday fun, too. Some people like to go on a picnic or to a soccer game. In *A Summer Birthday*, a boy and the United States have a birthday together. The Fourth of July is the birthday of the United States. What kind of a birthday party can you have for a country?

# A Summer Birthday

*Virginia A. Arnold*

Every summer Joshua could be found around the house looking sad. His birthday was on the Fourth of July. His mother said that his birthday was special because it was the birthday of the United States, too. Joshua didn't care much about that. He wanted his own birthday on his own day.

This time, before his birthday, his mother asked him, "What do you want for your birthday?"

Joshua said, "I don't know. Can we move my birthday to the winter?"

"Why do you want to do that?" asked his mother.

Joshua said, "Because what I want for my birthday is a birthday party with a birthday cake, presents, and friends. My friends from school go away over the Fourth of July. They can't come to my party. That is why I want to move my birthday."

"Joshua," said his mother, "if you want a birthday party, you will have one."

"But my friends from school . . ."
began Joshua.

His mother said, "If your school
friends are not around, why not look for
some new friends who are here. What
about Nicki Lin? Her father has a store
on this street."

"I know a new boy at day camp,"
said Joshua. "José moved here from
Puerto Rico this summer."

"What about Danielle and Tony?"
asked Joshua's mother. "They live right
up the street, too."

"They are bigger than I, but I like
them," said Joshua. "I don't know if all
these people will come to a birthday party
for me."

"You know how to find out," said
his mother.

So Joshua called all the children. He found out they all wanted to come. He said, "What about that? I am going to have a 'New Friends' birthday party. Where can we have the party? It's too hot in the house."

"We don't have a car, so it must be a place where we can walk or ride the bus," said his mother.

Joshua got out the map of the city and began to look for green places on it. Then he found the place he wanted. "We can go right up the street to the park," he said.

Later Joshua's mother said, "Tony's father called and asked if all of his family could come to your party. They asked if it could be a Fourth of July birthday party for you and the United States."

"Why not!" said Joshua.

Before long, every family wanted to come. "It's going to be a potluck party," said Joshua's mother.

"What is that?" asked Joshua.

"At a potluck party there is a collection of food. Each family brings its own food. Nicki's family brings Chinese food. Danielle's family brings French food. Tony's family brings a special Italian ice that his father is making. Then we will all eat together."

"I can see that we are going to eat on my birthday," said Joshua. "Will I get some presents, too?"

"We will see," said his mother.

The day of the party Joshua got up before the sun came up. He found his presents from his mother and father right by his bed. Grandma and Grandpa's presents were there, too. Joshua was happy. "I like my presents. Now on to the party," he said.

Joshua's father laughed and said, "Could we wait for the sun to come up?"

Before too long it was time to go to the park. Joshua and his friends played soccer and basketball. Then it was time to eat. "I like the . . . the . . . what is it called?" asked Joshua.

"It is called potluck," said his mother.

"That's it," said Joshua.

At last it was time for the birthday cake. It was a huge cake because it was for Joshua's birthday and for the birthday of the United States, too. On top of the cake Joshua found a special letter for him, and this is what it said:

Joshua got up and said, "I liked my Fourth of July birthday party. But what I will remember for a long, long time is my potluck birthday letter."

All his friends laughed and said, "Hurray for Joshua and for the U.S.A.!"

# Questions

Read and think.

1. Why didn't Joshua want his birthday to be on the Fourth of July?
2. Who wanted to come to Joshua's party?
3. Why did Joshua want to have the party in the park?
4. What is a potluck party?

# The Bears On Hemlock Mountain

*Alice Dalgliesh*

It was the year when Jonathan was eight that he went over Hemlock Mountain. He was a fine big boy for his age. That was why his mother could send him over the mountain all by himself.

Jonathan's mother sent him to his
Aunt Emma's to get a big iron pot
to cook stew in for a family party.
Jonathan made it over Hemlock
Mountain to his aunt's. After he'd had
a few cookies, he was so tired he fell
asleep. When he woke up, it was late
and so he started back up the mountain.
To keep up his courage, Jonathan said
to himself:

THERE *are*
  NO BEARS
    ON HEMLOCK MOUNTAIN,
NO BEARS AT ALL.
THERE ARE NO BEARS
    ON HEMLOCK MOUNTAIN,
NO BEARS, NO BEARS, NO BEARS,
  NO BEARS
    AT ALL.

Jonathan had gone quite a way before it suddenly came to him. He stood still in the snow, feeling very cross with himself. You and I know what he had forgotten.

THE BIG IRON POT!

There was nothing for poor Jonathan to do but to turn and go back.

How silly I am, he said to himself. How silly I am!

In a short time he was back at his Aunt Emma's house. Once more he lifted the brass knocker. Aunt Emma came to the door.

"Jonathan! Did you forget something?"

"I forgot what I came for," Jonathan said truthfully. "Mom sent me to ask for the loan of your big iron pot. All the aunts and uncles and cousins are coming to supper."

"And as I am one of them, I'll be glad to lend you my big iron pot," said Aunt Emma. She went into the kitchen and came back with the big iron pot. It was very large. Now Jonathan did not feel as if he had grown at least an inch. He felt like a very small boy.

"Do you think you can carry it?"

"Indeed I can," said Jonathan, trying to feel big and brave again. He took the pot by the handle and started off toward Hemlock Mountain.

When he was out of sight his aunt began to worry.

"He is not very big," she told the black cat. "And it is growing dark."

"Purr-rr-rr," said the black cat. "Purr-rr-rr."

"Oh, don't tell *me*," said Jonathan's aunt with crossness in her voice.

"YOU KNOW
    THERE MAY BE BEARS
        ON HEMLOCK MOUNTAIN!"

Jonathan and the big iron pot were going up the side of Hemlock Mountain.

Now it was really beginning to be dark. Jonathan knew he should hurry, but the iron pot was heavy. Jonathan's steps were heavy and slow. This time he was stepping in the big footprints he had made coming down.

It was really and truly dark. The tall trees were dark. The woods were dark and scary.

"Crack!" a branch broke in the woods. It was as loud as a pistol shot.

"Woo-ooh. Woo-ooh!" That was an owl, but it was a most lonely sound.

Jonathan began to think about bears. And to keep up his courage he said, in time to his own slow steps:

THERE . . . ARE . . . NO . . . BEARS
    ON . . . HEMLOCK . . . MOUNTAIN
NO BEARS . . . NO . . . BEARS . . .
AT . . . ALL.

He was tired and out of breath. So he rested for a minute, then he went on saying:

THERE . . . ARE . . . NO . . . BEARS . . .
    ON . . . HEMLOCK . . . MOUNTAIN.
    NO BEARS. . . .

Watch out, Jonathan. WATCH OUT! What was that, among the trees, right on top of the mountain? Two big, dark . . . what could they be?

They moved slowly . . . slowly . . .
but they were coming nearer . . . and
nearer . . . and nearer . . .

Jonathan had to think quickly.
There was only one thing to be done.
Jonathan did it. He put the big iron pot
upside down on the snow. Then he dug
out a place and crawled under it.

The pot was like a safe house. Jonathan dug out another little place in the snow so that he could breathe.

Then he waited.

Crunch! Crunch! Crunch. It was the sound of big, heavy paws on the snow.

The bears were coming!

Crunch! Crunch! Crunch! Nearer and nearer and nearer . . .

Jonathan's hair stood up straight on his head. He thought about a lot of things. He thought of his mother and father and the gray stone farmhouse.

Had they missed him? Would they come to look for him? He thought about the bears and wondered how they knew it was spring.

Crunch! Crunch! Crunch! Nearer and nearer . . . Jonathan made foolish words to the sound just to keep up his courage:

THERE . . . ARE . . . NO . . . BEARS
    ON . . . HEMLOCK . . . MOUNTAIN . . .
    NO . . . BEARS . . . AT . . . ALL . . .

But the sound had stopped. The bears were *right beside the big iron pot.*

Jonathan could hear them breathing.

And he was all alone on Hemlock Mountain.

---

*If you want to find out what happened to Jonathan, read the rest of* The Bears on Hemlock Mountain *by Alice Dalgliesh.*

# Glossary

# A

**a · bout**   You can learn <u>about</u> many things by looking at TV.

**af · ter**   Tim walked home <u>after</u> the basketball game.

**a · lone**   When Daniel left for school, his mother was all <u>alone</u>.

**an · i · mals**   Bears, birds, and fish are <u>animals</u>.

**ant**   Carmen looked at the <u>ant</u> walking over her foot.

**as**   The children in the race run <u>as</u> fast <u>as</u> they can.

# B

**bag**   Jack put the picnic food into a big, brown <u>bag</u>.

**bal · ance**   You must have good <u>balance</u> on the beam, or you will fall.

**beam**   The boys try to keep their balance walking on the <u>beam</u>.

**be · fore**   The girls will do the new dance step with the teacher <u>before</u> they try it alone.

**be · gan**   When night came, Amanda <u>began</u> to be scared.

**Ber · mu · da**   Many people live on the island of <u>Bermuda</u>.

**birth · day**   Your <u>birthday</u> is a special day.

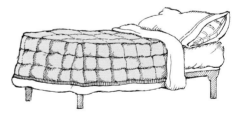

**blan · ket**   Mother put a warm <u>blanket</u> on the bed.

**blink · ing**   The car and the bus will stop at the <u>blinking</u> lights.

**blow**   The weather forecast says that it will rain and that the wind will <u>blow</u>.

**Bra·zil**   When it is summer in the United States, it is winter in <u>Brazil</u>.

**brings**   Every day Grandpa <u>brings</u> Emily eggs from his farm.

**build·ings**   There are many big <u>buildings</u> in a city.

**bump**   The plane came down with a <u>bump</u>.

**bus·y**   The bears are <u>busy</u> eating the fish.

# C

**cake**   Mother made a special <u>cake</u> for Nicki's birthday.

**camp·ing**   The family will take a tent and food when they go <u>camping</u>.

**cas·tles**   Not many people live in <u>castles</u> now.

**caught**   Maria <u>caught</u> the ball that flew through the air.

**cen·ti·me·ters**   The teacher asked Fred to measure the box in <u>centimeters</u>.

**Chi·na**   <u>China</u> is a huge country with many people.

**Chi·nese**   Debbie and her family like <u>Chinese</u> food.

**com·put·er**   There are many kinds of work a <u>computer</u> can do.

**cows**   We get milk from <u>cows</u>.

**crick · et**   Mark saw some boys playing a game of <u>cricket</u> when he was in England.

# D

**dair · y**   A truck will pick up milk at the <u>dairy</u> farm.

**Den · mark**   The country of <u>Denmark</u> is north of England.

**dif · fer · ent**   This street is too busy, so Ted will walk down a <u>different</u> street.

# E

**Eng · land**   Ben wanted to see many of the castles in <u>England</u>.

**Eng · lish**   People in this country had an <u>English</u> king at one time.

**ex · er · cis · es**   Swimming and running are good <u>exercises</u>.

# F

**feet**   "Your <u>feet</u> will get cold if you step in the snow," said Melissa.

**find**   Mother and Father help Ted <u>find</u> his missing sneakers.

**flood**   Water from a big rain may <u>flood</u> the land.

**fore · cast**   People on radio and TV <u>forecast</u> the weather so we can be ready for it.

**fore · cast · ers**   The weather <u>forecasters</u> say that there will be a big wind storm.

**231**

**found**   Lars lost the pictures, but then he <u>found</u> them.

**Fourth of Ju · ly**   The <u>Fourth of July</u> is the birthday of the United States.

**French**   Sally writes letters to her <u>French</u> friend.

**fun**   Chuckie and Amanda have <u>fun</u> when they play with their friends.

# G

**gauge**   Peggy can make a rain <u>gauge</u> to measure the rain.

**got**   Jason <u>got</u> the map to find the place where he was going.

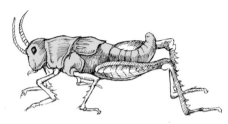

**grass · hop · per**   A <u>grasshopper</u> can jump very high.

**gym**   The children do exercises and play basketball in the <u>gym</u>.

**gym · nas · tics**   The <u>gymnastics</u> team will work on their exercises.

# H

**had**   John <u>had</u> his book when he left home.

**hard**   Running is <u>hard</u> work.

**has**   Irene <u>has</u> a new sweater.

**hear**   Tim and Tami <u>hear</u> their mother calling them to come home.

**hel · lo**   "<u>Hello</u>," said Bobby when he saw his teacher.

**here** "Are all the children here?" asked the teacher.

**him** Mike had a map with him when he went camping.

**hour** Father says, "Children, you may look at TV for one hour."

**how** How many claws does a cat have?

**hur·ri·cane** A hurricane is a big storm that can move from the water on to the land.

**is·land** There is water all around an island.

**I·tal·ian** Rita will learn to speak Italian from her grandma.

**I**

**ice** If it gets very cold, water may turn to ice.

**if** "If you make too much noise," said Mr. Miller, "the bird will fly away."

**im·por·tant** This is an important day, because we are going to the circus!

**inch·es** Do you know how many inches there are in a foot?

**J**

**join** The children asked Cuong to join their soccer team.

**joy** It was a joy for Lisa to dance.

**L**

**learn** Jeff will learn how to measure in both inches and centimeters.

**233**

**light·ning**   The children and their dog were scared of the thunder and lightning.

**line**   The children walk in a line from the school to the park.

**lodge**   A lodge is a kind of house.

**lunch**   The children had chicken for lunch.

# M

**ma·chines**   Machines help us do work.

**made**   José made a rain gauge from a can and a ruler.

**map**   Father looks at the map to see where he must drive.

**meas·ure**   Ben can measure his foot to see how long it is.

**milk**   Miko and Bart drink three glasses of milk every day.

**Mon·go·li·a**   Many people in Mongolia live in a tent.

# N

**no**   "No, thank you. I do not want to pet your dog," said Ben.

**noise**   Nan could not go to sleep because of all the noise.

**north**   Grandma and Grandpa live <u>north</u> of us.

**o·cean**   Many huge fish live in the <u>ocean</u>.

**our**   Ken and I take <u>our</u> pets camping with us.

**par·ty**   The children will go to the circus for Paul's birthday <u>party</u>.

**pi·lot**   A good <u>pilot</u> can fly a plane through a storm.

**place**   The park is a good <u>place</u> to run and play.

**plant**   The children and their teacher will walk through the buildings at the <u>plant</u> where sneakers are made.

**please**   "May I <u>please</u> keep the kitten for a pet?" asked Sam.

**pot·luck**   There were many kinds of food at the <u>potluck</u> picnic.

**Po·to·mac Riv·er**   A big boat can go in the <u>Potomac River</u> to Washington, D.C.

**pres·ents**   The twins thank their mother and father for all their birthday <u>presents</u>.

**pres·i·dent**   Do you know who the <u>president</u> of this country is?

**Puer·to Ri·co**   The people of <u>Puerto Rico</u> speak Spanish.

**queen**   Lisa read a story about a king and a <u>queen</u>.

**235**

# R

**ra·di·o**   You can turn on the radio when you want to know what the weather will be.

**rain**   The children had to stop playing soccer because of the rain.

**re·mem·ber**   Rosa and Katie have many pictures to help them remember their camping trips.

**re·port**   Father said, "Turn on the TV for the weather report."

**roared**   The lion roared when the cub played with his tail.

**roof**   A roof will keep rain out of the house.

**Roo·se·velt, The·o·dore**   Theodore Roosevelt was a president of the United States.

**rul·er**   You can use a ruler to measure or to make a line.

# S

**sat·el·lites**   Satellites can take pictures of the land from high in the air.

**scratch**   A bear can scratch with its claws.

**sing·ing**   The children were singing when they walked through the woods.

**skat·ing**   Ice skating is a hobby for many people.

**ski·ing**   Paco's family likes to go skiing in winter.

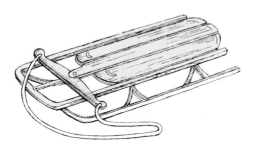

**sled**   Sue and Debbie ride over the snow on their sled.

**snow**   "You may play in the snow if you put on warm things," said Father.

**songs**   Jonathan is singing songs that the children like to hear.

**soon**   Soon after lunch, the children went swimming.

**space**   Satellites go around the world in space.

**Span·ish**   Anne and Jim learn to speak Spanish at school.

**speak**   In our country, many people speak both English and Spanish.

**splat**   The dog jumped into the water with a splat!

**spring**   In the spring, the weather is warm and the land is green.

**stars**   On some nights, you can see many stars in the sky.

**sta·tion**   Mark's father will pick him up at the bus station.

**storm**   When the storm is over, the children will go out to play.

**street**   Paco's house is on Park Street.

**strong**   Don can do many things because he is big and strong.

**stuck**   The box is <u>stuck</u> under the bed.

**sum · mer**   A hot day in the <u>summer</u> is a good time for a swim and a picnic.

**swamp**   A <u>swamp</u> is a very wet place.

**sweat · er**   Peggy put on a <u>sweater</u> because she was cold.

**sweeps**   Kirk <u>sweeps</u> the snow from the ice so he can go skating.

**Switz · er · land**   In the winter, there is much snow in <u>Switzerland</u>.

# T

**tell**   Mother and Father <u>tell</u> the babysitter where they will be.

**thank**   Rosa and Jim <u>thank</u> Mr. Green for the boat ride.

**these**   "Are <u>these</u> your glasses?" the teacher asked Eric.

**through**   The bird is flying <u>through</u> the air.

**thun · der**   First came the <u>thunder</u>, and then came the rain.

**trail**   "If we take this <u>trail</u>," said Ken, "we will come out of the woods."

**train**   The family will go to Washington, D.C., by <u>train</u>.

**trav · el**   The family will <u>travel</u> together on the boat.

**TV**   Pamela can see a play or a dance on TV.

## U

**U · nit · ed States**   Your country is called the United States.

## V

**vane**   A weather vane can tell where the wind is coming from.

**Vi · et · nam**   Cuong came to the United States from Vietnam.

## W

**Wash · ing · ton, D.C.**   Washington, D.C., is the home city of the president.

**weath · er**   In good weather, Martin and Jane can swim and play in the park.

**went**   David's family went on two trips last summer.

**wet**   If you go out in the rain, you will get wet.

**win · ter**   Winter is cold in the north of our country.

**Wis · con · sin**   Anne lives on a dairy farm in Wisconsin.

**world**   Mrs. Clark will see many new places on her trip around the world.

**wrote**   Ted wrote a letter to Kim and asked her to come to the city.

## Y

**yes**   "Yes, please," said Pilar, "I will have a drink of milk."

**239**